DALLAS
IMPRESSIONS
Photography by Jeremy Woodhouse

FARCOUNTRY
PRESS

Above: A nameplate outside Dallas City Hall bears the five-pointed star that also appears on the state flag of Texas, nicknamed the Lone Star State.

Right: From entrenched Fortune 500 companies to expanding homegrown businesses, Dallas reflects the entrepreneurial spirit.

Title page: Tulips invite visitors to enjoy the many dedicated gardens throughout the Dallas Arboretum's sixty-six acres on White Rock Lake.

Cover: "Live large. Think big." Dallas' slogan reflects a vibrant night scene.

Back cover: A Dallas landmark, the Pegasus sign sits atop the Magnolia Hotel.

ISBN 10: 1-56037-510-8
ISBN 13: 978-1-56037-510-4

© 2011 by Farcountry Press
Photography © 2011 by Jeremy Woodhouse

For more information about our books, write Farcountry Press, P.O. Box 5630, Helena, MT 59604; call (800) 821-3874; or visit www.farcountrypress.com.

Created, produced, and designed in the United States.
Printed in China.

16   15   14   13   12   11   1   2   3   4   5   6

Left: The John F. Kennedy Memorial, designed by famed American architect and Kennedy family friend Philip Johnson, offers a place for quiet contemplation.

Below, left: This inscription on the façade of the *Dallas Morning News* building was inspired by publisher G. B. Dealey's 1906 speech about the founders of the newspaper. The building, on downtown's Young Street, opened its doors in 1949.

Below, right: Pioneer Plaza's bronze depiction of a cattle drive, created by artist Robert Summers, commemorates the city's heritage by evoking the dusty nineteenth-century trails that led settlers to Dallas.

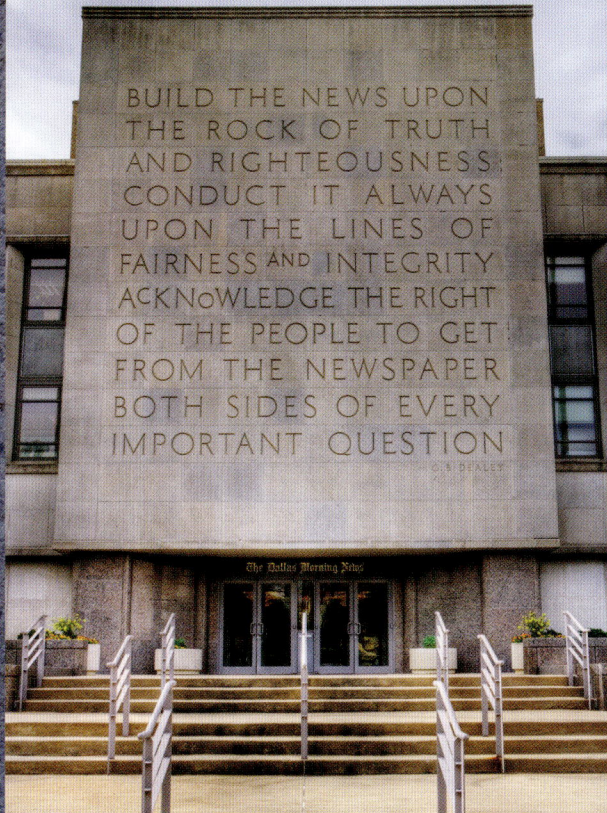

BUILD THE NEWS UPON THE ROCK OF TRUTH AND RIGHTEOUSNESS: CONDUCT IT ALWAYS UPON THE LINES OF FAIRNESS AND INTEGRITY ACKNoWLEDGE THE RIGHT OF THE PEOPLE TO GET FROM THE NEWSPAPER BOTH SIDES OF EVERY IMPORTANT QUESTION

The Dallas Morning News

Facing page: Among the amenities of the century-old Dallas Country Club, located in the community of Highland Park, is a 100-acre golf course with a view of the city skyline.

Below, left: Rancho Encinal is a forty-four-acre estate that was once the home of Everette DeGolyer, considered the "father of geophysics" and once the world's leading oil consultant. Located on the shores of White Rock Lake, DeGolyer's Spanish Colonial Revival house and surrounding landscaping—designed by landscape architects Arthur and Marie Berger—have been incorporated into the Dallas Arboretum and Botanical Gardens.

Below, right: The inviting lobby of the historic Adolphus Hotel has welcomed guests to its luxurious accommodations since 1912. It was once the tallest structure in Texas at twenty-one stories.

Above: Established in 1983, Dallas Area Rapid Transit (DART) efficiently transports locals and visitors to various venues in the greater Dallas area.

Facing page: The Dallas Farmers Market attracts shoppers to its tantalizing array of local produce, floral displays, and specialty foods. Certified local farmers find an enthusiastic market for their wares.

Above: Panes of lovely stained glass swirl heavenward in the Chapel of Thanks-Giving, part of Thanks-Giving Square, dedicated to the universal value of giving thanks for our blessings. Architect Philip Johnson designed the square and its attractions.

Right: Opened in 1982, the fifty-story glass skyscraper known as the Thanksgiving Tower—adjacent to Thanks-Giving Square—was once the second-tallest building in Dallas.

Left: With its tenth-floor swimming pool and other comforts, The Joule hotel pampers its guests after a day spent enjoying local attractions and shopping.

Below: Folks looking for funky fashion and trendy bars might visit Deep Ellum, a renovated warehouse district located just a few blocks east of downtown Dallas.

Above, left: The entrance to the Dallas Zoo is marked by a sculpted giraffe reaching up for a leafy snack with its long tongue. Designed by St. Louis architect Bob Cassilly, the giraffe is the tallest statue in Dallas at more than sixty-seven feet.

Above, center: A gorilla surveys his surroundings from his naturalistic enclosure at the zoo.

Above, right: A couple of defunct warehouses in downtown Dallas were gutted, then transformed with a unique display of flora and fauna into the Dallas World Aquarium.

Facing page: The Dallas Zoo's monorail takes visitors on a one-mile safari tour through the Wilds of Africa exhibit, enabling up-close viewing of the wildlife in the six African habitats.

Left: Reunion Tower, one of Dallas' most familiar landmarks, allows spectacular views of the sparkling nightscape. The tower's rotating top floor offers fine dining.

Below: A haven only minutes away from downtown Dallas, the Trinity River Audubon Center serves as the gateway to the 6,000-acre Great Trinity Forest. The LEED-certified (a rating system that evaluates efficiency) center offers educational hands-on exhibits, seasonal programs, and the Children's Discovery Garden.

Above, left: An impressive spire and distinctive clock have made the Mercantile Bank Building a landmark since 1943. Oil tycoon H. L. Hunt had his business in this building, which was the only Dallas skyscraper erected during World War II.

Above, right: A plane lands at Dallas/Fort Worth International Airport.

Far right: Boasting a fine view of the Dallas skyline, the Delmont Hotel was constructed in 1946 at the then impressive sum of $400,000. It was one of the first hotels to offer year-round air conditioning.

Above: Corridor Pin, a whimsical sculpture of an upside-down safety pin by Claes Oldenburg and Coosje van Bruggen, is just one of several pieces of world-class art at NorthPark Center, a premier shopping center in Dallas.

Left: As the Dallas skyline slips into dusk, its vibrant nightlife gets underway.

Following pages: Photographed from the Triple Underpass, Dealey Plaza is the infamous location of President John F. Kennedy's assassination on November 22, 1963. The Texas School Book Depository is the building at the far left of the image, and in front of it is the famed Grassy Knoll. Visitors to Dealey Plaza can also tour the recently restored Old Red Courthouse, pictured at the center right.

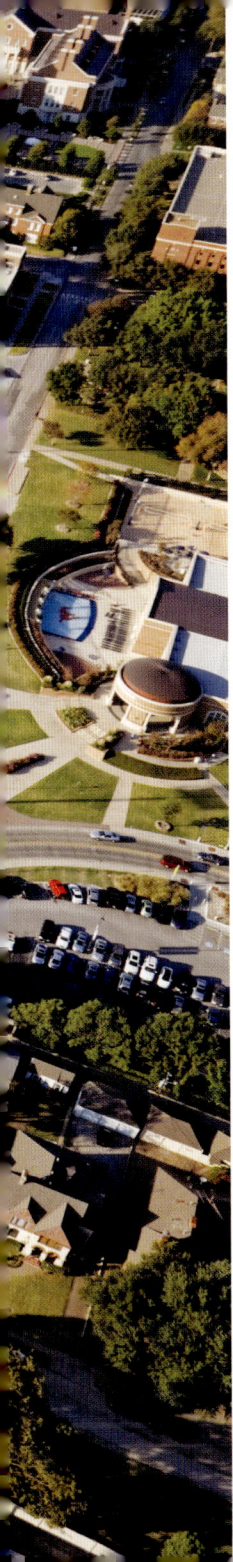

Left: Located near the heart of Dallas, Southern Methodist University embraces both academics and athletic pursuits. The Ford Stadium is home to the SMU Mustangs.

Below: A copper dome brings distinction to the first building erected on the campus of private college SMU. Dallas Hall was named in honor of local citizens and philanthropists who supported its construction.

Right: Linking Dallas' major freeways, the High Five Interchange, a mammoth five-level structure of concrete, took four years to complete and transports more than 500,000 commuters daily.

Below, left: The Dallas skyline provides a backdrop for scores of fresh blooms at the Dallas Farmers Market.

Below, right: Entrepreneurs Neiman and Marcus joined forces in the early 1900s to create the flagship store of a successful chain. The store at Main and Ervay is lavishly decorated for the holidays, and the unveiling of its themed window displays draws large crowds.

Above: The Meadows Museum reopened in 2009 following a renovation of its plaza and sculpture garden. Spanish artist Jaume Plensa created a striking centerpiece: a ten-foot stainless-steel sculpture called *Sho*, inspired by a portrait of a young Chinese girl.

Left: Symmetrical townhouses share the neighborhood with the Dallas Museum of Art, designed by architect Edward Larrabee Barnes, as well as the Morton H. Meyerson Symphony Center, created by prize-winning architect I. M. Pei.

Facing page: Modern touches abound in the state-of-the-art Margot and Bill Winspear Opera House. Its principal performance hall seats more than 2,000 patrons and features world-class acoustics.

Below, left: This Pegasus-emblazoned sign invites visitors to stroll through the downtown Dallas Arts District, an area first envisioned by city leaders in the 1970s and now one of the largest urban arts districts in the country.

Below, center: Although originally established in 1903, the current Dallas Museum of Art moved to the arts district in 1984.

Below, right: The Trammell and Margaret Crow Collection of Asian Art in the Trammell Crow Center beckons art lovers to peruse its galleries of fine art at no charge.

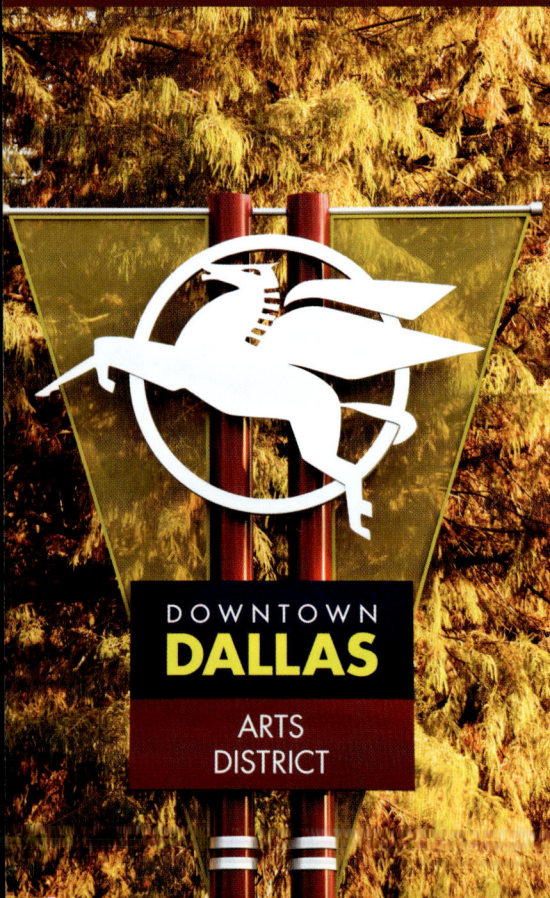

Left: A variety of attractive trees shade the large-scale sculptures throughout the gardens of the Nasher Sculpture Center. Patsy and Raymond Nasher began their extensive art collection in the 1950s.

Below: The Nashers also founded one of the first U.S. malls; ribbon-cutting for NorthPark Center occurred in 1965.

Right: Cotton baron Sheppard W. King built the palatial 10,000-square-foot home known today as Rosewood Mansion on Turtle Creek. Its famous houseguests include President Franklin Roosevelt and playwright Tennessee Williams, who wrote *Summer and Smoke* while staying here.

Below, left: Potential Dallas homebuyers will find a wide variety of luxury apartments, condos, and townhouses in uptown Dallas.

Below, right: The well-known icon of a leaping greyhound marks the bus line's headquarters on North St. Paul Street.

Following pages: Residents of the Manor House Apartments, which opened in 1966, enjoy panoramic views of downtown Dallas.

Facing page: Big Tex, a fifty-two-foot cowboy figure erected in the middle of the fairgrounds in 1952, wears size-seventy boots and a seventy-five-gallon hat. His hinged jaw allows him to appear to make announcements.

Below, left: The Texas Hall of State, built in 1936 as a monument to Texas' rich history, houses the Dallas Historical Society. It is located at Fair Park, which hosts the Texas State Fair each fall and also features a number of interesting museums.

Below, center: The Texas Star Ferris Wheel, imported from Italy, carries riders some twenty stories high during the fair, which draws more than three million visitors each year.

Below, right: This fair lady is one of six flanking the entrance to the Hall of State.

The Cathedral Shrine of the Virgin of Guadalupe, located in the Dallas Arts District, boasts one of the largest congregations in the country with 25,000 families. The church, a fine example of High Victorian Gothic architecture, offers services in both Spanish and English.

Above: Dallas Cowboys quarterback Tony Romo looks for a receiver in a game against the Tennessee Titans. The Cowboys formed as a franchise in 1960. © CORBIS/RAY CARLIN/ICON SMI

Right: Completed in 2009 at a cost of more than $1 billion, the Cowboys Stadium seats 80,000 fans and is the largest domed stadium with a retractable roof in the world.

Above, left: The W Dallas - Victory Hotel offers Texas-sized hospitality to its guests with posh bars, an infinity pool, a spa, complete in-room services, and spectacular views of the city.

Above, right: Modernism finds expression in this downtown glass high-rise called the Hunt Oil Tower, home to the Hunt Oil Corporation.

Left: Victory Park, a planned urban development, lies northwest of downtown. The American Airlines Center, a multi-purpose arena, was its first tenant and is home to the NBA's Dallas Mavericks and the NHL's Dallas Stars.

Above: The swimming pool at The Joule, a luxurious downtown hotel, extends eight feet outside the building and features a glass window at the end.

Right: Spanish architect and engineer Santiago Calatrava was commissioned by Southern Methodist University to design a sculpture for the Meadows Museum. The resulting creation, a series of hollow bars called *Wave*, rises and descends over a reflecting pool.

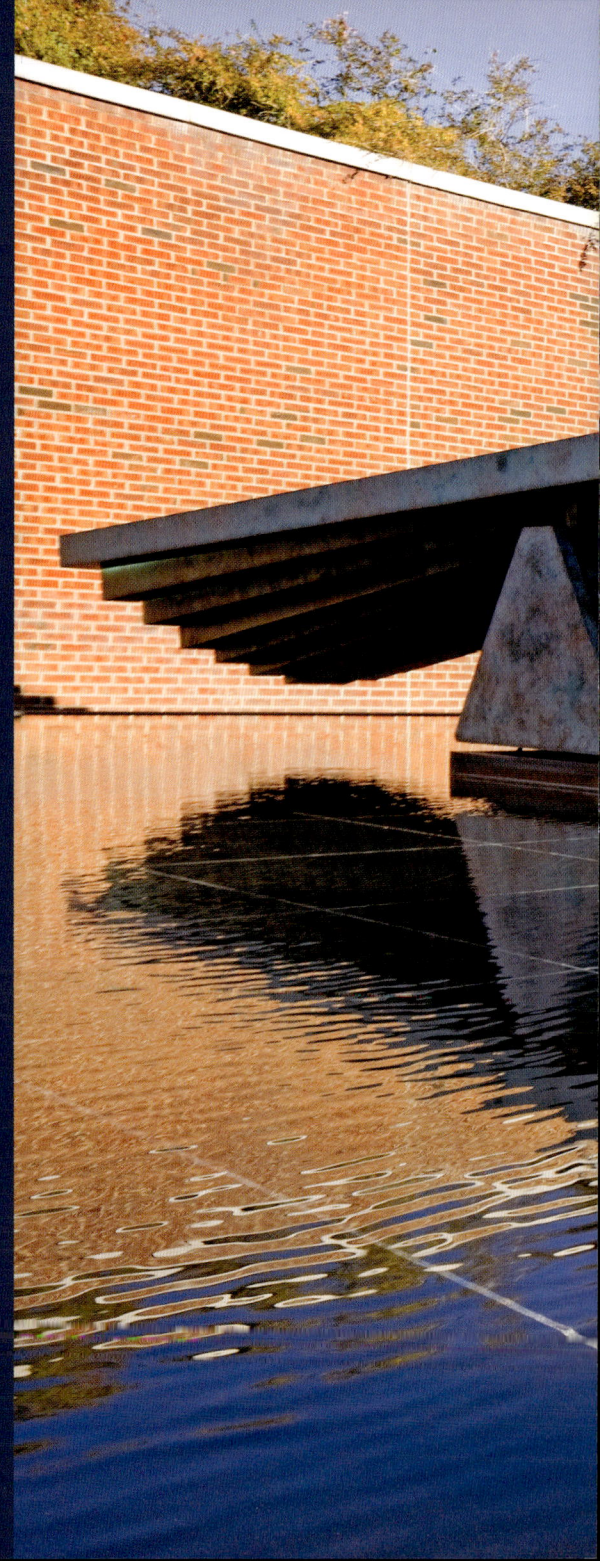

Left: Shoppers can take a break to enjoy ice skating under a vaulted glass ceiling in Galleria Dallas, an upscale shopping mall with more than 200 stores.

Below: A spiral staircase is one of the many appealing Baroque-inspired features inside the Morton H. Meyerson Symphony Center.

Above: Fans watch a baseball game at Rangers Ballpark. The Rangers team won its first American League Pennant in the fall of 2010.

Right: Rangers Ballpark incorporates a retro-style design with many features reminiscent of other famous ballparks. The exterior façades are made of brick and Texas "sunset red" granite. Players consider it a "hitter-friendly" ballpark.

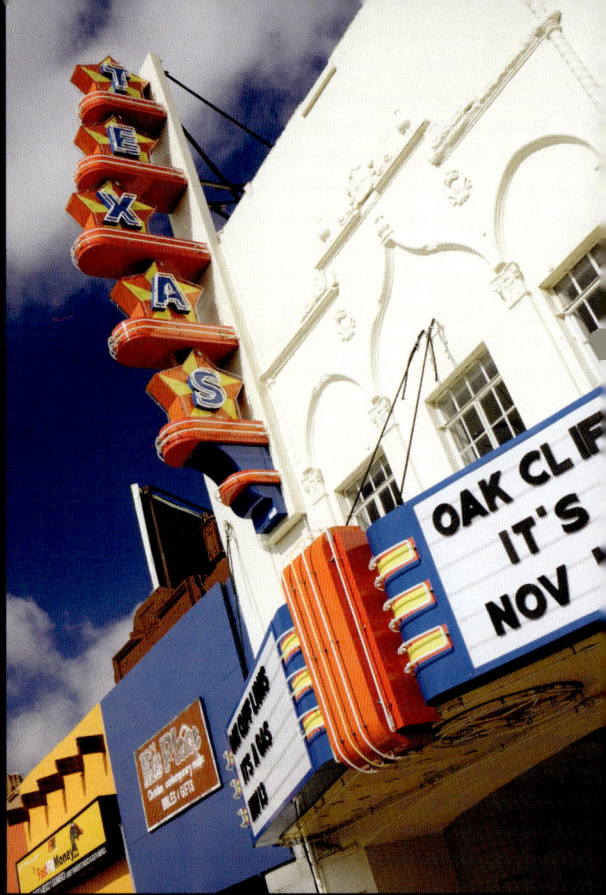

The circa 1920 Majestic Theatre, the last of the movie houses on Dallas' Theatre Row, staged vaudeville acts before hosting silver screen premieres and big band performances. Today the theater hosts a variety of musical and performing acts.

Although the Texas Theatre opened in 1931 with modern acoustics and equipment, it is infamous as the place where Dallas police converged to arrest Lee Harvey Oswald. Today the community-run theater looks to local support to keep its doors open.

World War II–weary Americans flocked to theaters such as the Inwood Theatre, whose innovative marine murals, painted nymphs on the ceiling, and unique pay phone in a large shell delighted patrons. Present-day foreign-language and independent films as well as a busy martini bar keep guests coming.

For more than sixty years, audiences at the Granada Theater have enjoyed memorable films and live music. Its state-of-the-art sound system complements the theater's original décor.

Above, left: Infomart, one of Dallas' largest and most distinctive structures, was inspired by England's Crystal Palace, which was constructed in London for the Great Exhibition of 1851. More than 100 technology and telecommunications companies are housed here.

Above, right: The brick towers of the aptly named Old Red Museum, built in 1892 as a courthouse, are juxtaposed with the modern fifty-story Reunion Tower in a blend of different architectural eras.

Right: Viewers of the *Dallas* television series will remember this familiar cityscape, including the multitiered Hyatt Regency Dallas and the Reunion Tower.

Visitors to the Dallas Heritage Village in Old City Park stroll through the village to learn about the history of North Texas from 1840 to 1910. Costumed guides provide a glimpse of early prairie life in the village's thirty-eight restored structures, including a Civil War–era farm, a print shop, a general store, and a saloon.

Right: The trademark neon Pegasus sign initially rotated above the 1922-era Magnolia Petroleum Company. The original sign resides at the Dallas Farmers Market, but a new sign on the renovated Magnolia Hotel now welcomes guests to the upscale establishment.

Below, left: For more than fifty years, the Mesquite Championship Rodeo's fast horses, gutsy cowboys and cowgirls, and silly clowns have thrilled and entertained visitors.

Below, right: The Bank of America building, the tallest building in Dallas, was one of the first structures in the United States to receive the Energy Star award for efficiency. The sculpture *Venture* stands outside on the plaza.

Left: The Dallas skyline serves as a backdrop for a blur of car lights wending their way to and from downtown on I-30.

Below: Construction on the 1.5-mile Texas Motor Speedway began in 1995. The track has since seen many exciting finishes. Car shows, bands, and a new drag strip also attract fans to the venue.
PHOTO COURTESY DENNIS FRITSCHE, DENNISFRITSCHE.COM.

Above, left: A bronze sculpture in West End known as *San Antonio Rose* commemorates the life of Bob Wills, known as "King of Western Swing." Native Texan William Easley created this memorial as well as a number of other tributes to Lone Star State musical celebrities in the same area.

Above, right: A rather ordinary building, the Texas School Book Depository became a tragic part of American history on November 22, 1963, when President John F. Kennedy was assassinated. The Sixth Floor Museum chronicles the events of this fateful day.

Facing page: Artist Robert Glen designed and oversaw the creation of the largest equestrian sculpture in the world. Small fountains in the pool at the feet of the mustangs at Las Colinas give the appearance of horses splashing through a stream.

Left: One of Dallas' signature skyscrapers, the Chase Tower features a curved glass roof and a 1.5-acre landscaped plaza.

Below, left: Visitors to the Crow Collection of Asian Art in the Trammell Crow Center learn about the influence of Asian art and culture on the rest of the world. The distinguished collection features pieces spanning thousands of years.

Below, right: Although partially obscured by larger skyscrapers, the Magnolia Hotel invites guests to appreciate its historic façade and modern interior.

Following pages: Life in downtown Dallas doesn't set with the sun. Countless fine restaurants and hip bars, upscale shopping venues, and exciting cultural events mean there's something to do every night of the week.

Left: Opened the same day as the Texas State Fair in 1916, the Beaux Arts–style Union Terminal served as a focal point for the passenger rail stations in Dallas. Today Union Station serves a variety of transportation functions and hosts catered private events as well.

Below: Utilizing 3.1 million square feet, the Dallas World Trade Center offers everything from a post office to stores with gifts and home furnishings. A unique display of flags from around the world is located on the ground floor.

Facing page: A reflecting pool and plaza at the Dallas City Hall provide a relaxing respite from the harried daily life of downtown Dallas.

Below, left: The Dallas Piece, a sculpture by world-famous British artist Henry Moore, graces the plaza of the Dallas City Hall.

Below, right: Many a cutting-edge band has performed in Deep Ellum, an arts and entertainment district in east Dallas.

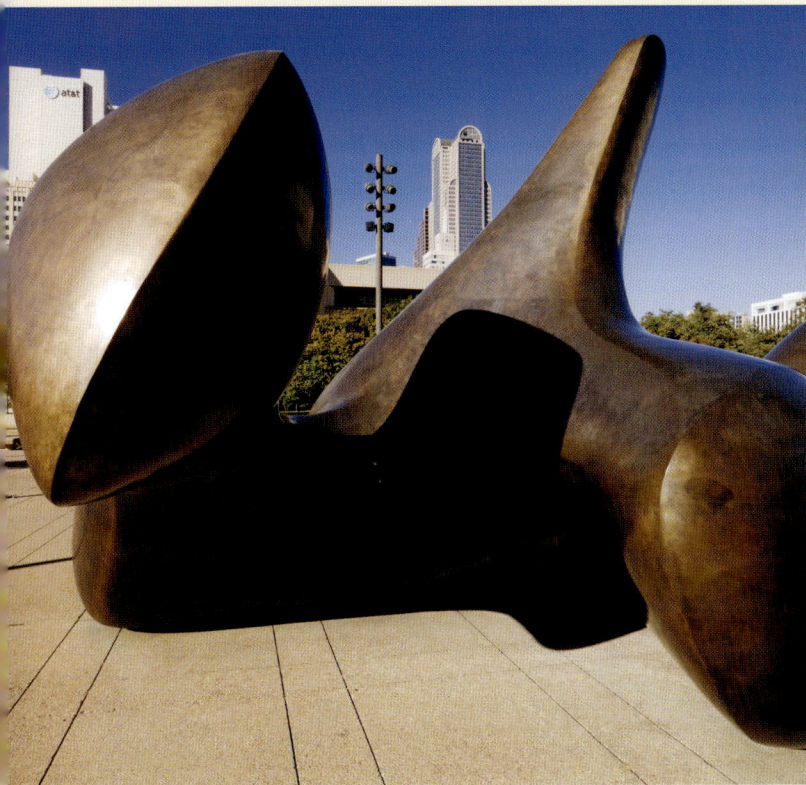

Above: Opened in January 1997, the Mockingbird DART (Dallas Area Rapid Transit) station is located in the densely populated neighborhood around the intersection of Mockingbird Lane and US 75 North Central Expressway.

Right: Renowned architect I. M. Pei designed Dallas' modern and distinctive City Hall. The inverted pyramid design seems to be supported by three enormous pillars, but they actually contain stairwells and are not weight-bearing.

Left: The green argon lighting of the Bank of America building and the flashing globe of the Reunion Tower bring flair to the Dallas skyline.

Below: A black granite reflecting pool outside the Winspear Opera House is only part of the attractive outdoor features linking the various venues of the AT&T Performing Arts Center.

Right: Five-pointed stars were cast into the concrete support columns of the High Five Interchange.

Below: A visit to Kuby's Sausage House in Snider Plaza isn't complete without picking up some items from the supermarket and deli to enjoy later.

Jeremy Woodhouse is an outdoor photographer based in Dallas, Texas. He spends much of each year on the road, photographing landscapes, cityscapes, and wildlife. For the past five years he has led photographic tours to destinations such as Japan, Italy, and Mexico.

He worked as a freelance graphic designer in the United Kingdom, South Africa, and the United States before he began living his dream of being a full-time professional stock photographer in 1998. Whether he's photographing a flock of red-crowned cranes in a winter landscape in Japan or capturing the last light as it falls on the Dallas skyline, Jeremy brings a designer's eye to the composition and creation of all his images.

Jeremy's photos have appeared in print all over the world. He has received numerous international awards in the Wildlife Photographer of the Year Competition, and he was overall winner of the 2002 Nature's Best International Photography Awards. His images have been included in exhibitions at the Smithsonian in Washington, D.C., the Dallas Museum of Natural History, and the Natural History Museum in London.